1 Introduction

How do consumers form inflation expectations and what determines their forecast accuracy? These questions are of critical importance for central banks and macroeconomists, since inflation expectations are known to affect the actual evolution of inflation and macroeconomy more generally. Recognizing this importance, central banks have in recent decades devoted considerable effort to anchoring inflation expectations, for instance, by announcing inflation targets. Consumer inflation expectations have also been central in explaining the evolution of inflation in the aftermath of the financial crisis, first during the period of the "missing disinflation" (during which inflation was higher than would have been expected based on models with standard determinants like the magnitude of the output gap and inflation expectations of professional forecasters) and subsequently, when inflation was weaker than expected (Coibion and Gorodnichenko, 2015; Friedrich, 2014). However, while a substantial body of empirical research has extensively studied professional forecasters' inflation expectations (among many others, see Capistran and Timmermann, 2009; Coibion and Gorodnichenko, 2010), much less is known about expectations by the households.

Consumer expectations are known to be biased and inefficient, with forecast errors being systematically correlated with demographic characteristics (Souleles, 2004). They are also affected by frequently purchased items, such as gasoline, as pointed out recently by Coibion and Gorodnichenko (2015), and they are responsive to media reporting (Carroll, 2003). In addition to these factors, the current paper tests whether consumer attitudes also shape inflation expectations. We find that consumers who are pessimistic about their economic or financial situation are likely to have higher inflation expectations. When consumers struggle to make ends meet with their available budget, it may be due to a reduction in their income or to an increase in their expenditures – which in turn could be due to several factors, one of them being rising prices for their consumption bundle. Under uncertain information and information-processing constraints, it might well be that such consumers estimate inflation to be higher than others. In addition, it has been shown that financially constrained consumers are more attentive to price changes of the goods they purchase than more affluent consumers (Snir and Levy, 2011). Combining this with the well-known notion that agents are more receptive to bad than to good news (see, e.g., Baumeister, Bratslavsky, Finkenauer, and Vohs, 2001) might well imply that financially constrained consumers arrive at a higher estimate of inflation.

The paper uses more than 175,000 observations from the Surveys of Consumers conducted by University of Michigan over the years 1980 to 2011 to test these hypotheses. We find that consumers with pessimistic attitudes about major purchases (such as purchases of durables, houses or vehicles), who find themselves in difficult financial situations, or who expect income to go down in the future do indeed have a stronger upward bias in their inflation expectations. Also NBER recessions (another proxy for consumer pessimism and their financial difficulties) are associated with an incremental bias in inflation expectations.

We also confirm the earlier findings that consumers are responsive to news. We employ two news measures, the first based on the survey itself (where respondents can report whether they have recently heard news about prices), and the second, following Carroll (2003), based on intensity of news coverage related to inflation in the *New York Times* and the *Washington Post*. While both of these measures have been used previously, e.g., in Pfajfar and Santoro (2013), how they differ, and how each of them would have to be interpreted, have not been discussed. In this paper, we clarify that reporting having heard news about prices is very tightly linked to gasoline price inflation in the United States. This relationship is in line with earlier evidence that frequently purchased items (such as gasoline) shape the inflation perceptions of consumers, and also likely reflects the fact that gasoline prices are extremely salient due to their prominent postings at gas stations.

Interestingly, our two news measures have very different implications for consumer inflation expectations. Having heard news about prices (reflecting predominantly large increases in gasoline prices) increases the bias. In contrast, more intense media coverage tends to reduce the bias and improve forecast accuracy. In that regard, consumers with more strongly upward-biased expectations are more responsive to media coverage, and see their bias shrinking by more than the other consumer groups.

These findings have interesting implications for policy-makers and the media, suggesting that more reporting about inflation improves consumers' inflation expectations, and particularly so for consumers who are in the right tail of the distribution, i.e., have a particularly strong upward bias.

The paper connects to the previous literature on the determinants of consumer inflation expectations. In that regard, a number of factors have been identified that shape the *level* of inflation expectations. Several socio-economic characteristics are known to affect inflation expectations – females tend to have higher inflation expectations than men, and inflation expectations tend to decrease with income, whereas they are often found to be lower for older consumers (Jonung, 1981; Bryan and Venkatu, 2001; Lombardelli and Saleheen, 2003; Christensen, Els, and Rooij, 2006; Anderson, 2008). These socio-economic determinants of inflation expectations are rather stable over time, which makes it hard to explain why household inflation expectations, their accuracy and the magnitude of their bias are subject to substantial time variation (Coibion and Gorodnichenko, 2015). The current paper suggests a time-varying characteristic, consumer attitudes, that can help addressing this. A small number of related studies have provided some evidence in that direction. Webley and Spears (1986) show that U.K. consumers who think they have done less well financially than during the previous year, as well as consumers who expect to be worse off in the subsequent year, have higher inflation expectations. Similarly, del Giovane, Fabiani, and Sabbatini (2009) and Malgarini (2009) find that inflation expectations of Italian consumers are higher for respondents with pessimistic attitudes, and for consumers in financial difficulties.

Inflation expectations are also determined by the inflation that consumers actually experience – first, inflation expectations are shaped much more by the inflation rate of consumption baskets that relate to the respective socio-economic group to which the individual belongs than by the overall inflation indices, at least for low-education and low-income consumers (Pfajfar and Santoro, 2009; Menz and Poppitz, 2013); second, inflation expectations vary positively with the inflation experience that individuals have undergone over their lifetime (Lombardelli and Saleheen, 2003; Malmendier and Nagel, 2013); third, more frequently purchased items have been found to have a higher impact on inflation perceptions and inflation expectations (Ranyard, Missier, Bonini, Duxbury, and Summers, 2008; Georganas, Healy, and Li, 2014).

The *evolution* of consumers' inflation expectations has also been studied. In his seminal paper, Carroll (2003) has demonstrated that consumers update their expectations only infrequently (roughly once every year), that they respond to media reporting and update toward the expectations of professional forecasters, and that inattention to news generates stickiness in aggregate inflation expectations. Subsequently, a number of contributions have studied the role of media reporting for inflation expectations in more detail. Lamla and Maag (2012) analyze the effect of media reporting on disagreement among forecasters, and find professional forecaster disagreement to be unaffected by media coverage, whereas disagreement among households increases with higher and more diverse media coverage. Pfajfar and Santoro (2009) provide evidence that the effect of news on inflation expectations differs across socio-economic groups, and Easaw, Golinelli, and Malgarini (2013) demonstrate that the rate at which professional forecasts are embodied in households' expectations depends on socio-economic characteristics. Finally, Pfajfar and Santoro (2013) highlight the importance of differentiating between media reporting on inflation and whether a consumer has actually heard news about prices. Their study replicates Carroll's finding that inflation expectations get updated *toward* the professional forecasts using aggregate data. However, this is not the case at the individual consumer level, where most consumers who update actually revise their expectations *away* from the professional benchmark, but by sufficiently small amounts that they are dominated in the aggregate data by relatively few consumers who update toward professional forecasts by large amounts. Differences in the magnitude of revisions that take place in response to news have been identified by Armantier, Nelson, Topa, van der Klaauw, and Zafar (2012), who find larger revisions for agents that start off with relatively less precise expectations. These findings are in line with the current paper, which suggests that media reporting about inflation improves inflation expectations particularly for consumers who are in the right tail of the distribution, i.e., have a particularly strong upward bias.

The remainder of the paper is structured as follows. In Section 2, we describe the data used in our empirical analysis and provide some stylized facts. Section 3 provides an overview of the econometric approach that we employ, while Section 4 reports the relevant results. Section 5 concludes.

2   The Data and Some Descriptive Analysis

Our microdata contain information on a wide range of factors that influence consumers' inflation expectations. As such, they allow us to explore households' forecast accuracy in great detail. In this section we describe the key features of the data set and report some preliminary evidence on consumers' inflation expectations, as well as on the newspaper index proposed by Carroll and a direct measure of consumers' receptiveness toward news on prices. Moreover, we report some descriptive statistics about consumer-level characteristics that are accounted for as determinants of the process of expectations formation.

Photo Rmoved Due to Copyright Restrictions

Notes: The chart reports the University of Michigan, Surveys of Consumers (MS) and the Survey of Professional Forecasters conducted by the Federal Reserve Bank of Philadelphia (SPF) mean forecasts for inflation at $t + 12$, as well as inflation as realized at $t + 12$. Based on monthly data. Source: University of Michigan, Surveys of Consumers and Survey of Professional Forecasters, Federal Reserve Bank of Philadelphia.

2.1 Inflation Expectations

The Survey of Consumer Attitudes and Behavior is a representative survey conducted monthly by the Survey Research Center at the University of Michigan (Curtin, 2013). Participants in the Surveys of Consumers (henceforth, MS) are asked two questions about expected changes in prices: first, whether they expect prices to go up, down or stay the same in the next 12 months; second, to provide a quantitative statement about the expected change.[1]

The analysis will focus on the 1980M1-2011M12 period. Figure 1 reports the mean forecasts obtained in the MS against CPI inflation.[2] To provide another benchmark, the figure also includes forecasts from the Survey of Professional Forecasters (SPF), a survey among leading private forecasting firms that is currently conducted by the Federal Reserve Bank of Philadelphia.[3] Both the MS and the SPF appear to predict inflation reasonably well, although they often fail to match periods of low inflation. For instance, at the very end of the sample, from 2009-11, they are considerably higher than actual inflation turned out to be. This episode has been studied by Coibion and Gorodnichenko (2015), who suggest that, due to high oil price inflation, household inflation expectations were elevated, which in turn helps explain the "missing disinflation" in the United States (i.e., the fact that standard Phillips curves would have predicted a disinflation over that period that did not materialize).

2.2 News on Inflation

A direct implication of Carroll's view is that more media reporting should imply that people are better informed and produce better forecasts. To account for this possibility, we require reliable indicators of the flow of news on inflation that the public is confronted with. Carroll computes a yearly index of the intensity of news coverage in the *New York Times* and the *Washington Post*. In this paper, we use the monthly version of this index that has been constructed in Pfajfar and Santoro (2013). It is based on a search of each of the two newspapers for inflation-related articles, converted into an index by dividing the

---

[1]If a respondent expects prices to stay the same, the interviewer must make sure that the respondent does not actually expect that prices will change at the same rate at which they have changed over the past 12 months. In line with common practice, we discard observations if the respondent expects inflation to be less than -5% or more than +30%. This rule only affects 0.7% of the observations in the sample under scrutiny. Curtin (1996) also adopts alternative truncation intervals, such as [-10%,50%], showing that the key statistical properties of the resulting sample are close to invariant across different cut-off rules.

[2]Inflation expectations sampled at time t are graphed with inflation 12 months later, so as to be in line with the forecast target.

[3]The SPF is a quarterly survey. In order to obtain a monthly estimate of the SPF we may consider two options: either forecasters keep their forecast until the next survey round, or their "monthly" forecast includes a partial adjustment to the next quarter forecast. We took both approaches and obtained nearly identical results. This paper is based on a linear interpolation of the data.

number of inflation-related articles by the total number of articles.[4] To be more precise, we define this news measure as $NEWS_t^N = 100\frac{n_t}{N_t} - \overline{NEWS}^N$, where n_t denotes the number of inflation-related articles in a given month t, N_t the total number of articles, and $\overline{NEWS}^N$ the sample average of the news measure. We demean the news measure to allow for an easier interpretation of interaction terms in the regression analysis.

In addition, our analysis will rely on a measure of consumers' perceptions of new information about prices. This is intended to complement the newspaper index proposed by Carroll. In fact, the accuracy of a proxy based on the intensity of news coverage in national newspapers can be questioned on different grounds. For instance, Blinder and Krueger (2004) suggest that consumers primarily rely on information about inflation from television, followed by local and national newspapers. It is also plausible to expect that the volume of news about inflation does not necessarily match the flow of information that is assimilated by the public. In this respect, a non-trivial discrepancy could result from the interplay of two mutually reinforcing effects: (i) news from the media does not necessarily reach the public uniformly and (ii) the connection between news and inflation expectations is likely to be affected by consumers' receptiveness to the news and the capacity to process new information. Indeed, Sims (2003) emphasizes the presence of information-processing constraints that could be compatible with such inefficiencies. Finally, it is well known that consumer inflation perceptions are shaped – in line with the availability heuristic (Tversky and Kahneman, 1974) – by frequently purchased items (Ranyard, Missier, Bonini, Duxbury, and Summers, 2008), such that in periods where inflation of such items is high, consumers might be more aware and concerned about inflation, whereas media reporting (which most likely is generally concerned with overall inflation) need not be more intense.

In light of these considerations, it is advisable to complement the analysis with a variable that accounts for consumers' actual perceptions of inflation. Such a variable is directly available from the MS, where respondents are asked whether they have heard of any changes in business conditions during the previous few months. In case of an affirmative response, the respondents have the possibility to give two types of news that they have heard about, among them being either higher or lower prices. Our second news variable, $NEWS_i^P$, is therefore defined as a dummy variable that takes the value of one

---

[4]A potential problem connected with this type of search is that the resulting index may include articles that do not primarily cover U.S. inflation. Accordingly, Pfajfar and Santoro (2013) tested the robustness of this methodology by restricting the search to articles that just cover U.S. inflation, and found the results to be robust.

if the respondent cites prices as a factor that has come to their attention.[5]

Photo Rmoved Due to Copyright Restrictions

Notes: The chart reports CPI inflation as recorded for a given time period t, as well as the share of respondents in the MS in period t answering that they have heard news about prices ("perceived news") and the index about media reporting related to inflation in period t ("news stories"). Based on monthly data. Source: University of Michigan, Surveys of Consumers.

Figure 2 reports the fraction of MS respondents who have heard news about prices, together with the newspaper index and CPI inflation. The two series display poor correlation, suggesting that they contain two distinct measures of news. The fraction of MS respondents who have heard news about prices exhibit more volatility than the newspaper index. Especially in the latter part of the sample it displays sizable fluctuations that neither actual inflation nor the newspaper index presents. Splitting the series into the share of respondents who have heard news about decreasing and increasing prices, respectively, it is evident that most of the volatility in the overall series arises due to

---

[5]The MS respondents primarily report about news on unemployment, followed by news on the government (elections) and then prices. It is important to stress that 41% of the respondents report having heard no news at all and that in 28% of the cases only one type of news is reported. This is to say that, on average, only 31% of the respondents are confronted with a potentially binding limit of two options. Therefore, though some underreporting may affect our measure of perceived news about prices, this is not likely to be primarily induced by the specific design of the questionnaire.

movements in the share of consumers who have heard about rising prices (see Figure 3).

Photo Rmoved Due to Copyright Restrictions

Notes: The chart reports CPI inflation as recorded for a given time period t, as well as the share of respondents in the MS in period t answering that they have heard about prices increasing / decreasing. Based on monthly data. Source: University of Michigan, Surveys of Consumers.

So what is behind this measure of news? As shown in Figure 4, the correlation between the share of respondents reporting that they have heard about price increases and inflation of retail gasoline prices is very high (0.63).[6] Based on this evidence, we interpret the survey-based news measure as capturing inflation perceptions originating from frequently-purchased items such as gasoline prices. In contrast, the correlation between negative inflation rates in gasoline prices and the share of respondents reporting that they have heard about decreases is much smaller (0.23), which is in line with the prospect theory pioneered by Kahneman and Tversky (1979), since agents tend to manifest higher receptiveness toward "bad" news on prices, as compared with "good" news.

---

[6]For Figure 4, we set any negative gasoline inflation numbers to zero, to reflect the fact that the survey news measure only reflects having heard about price *increases*.

9

Photo Rmoved Due to Copyright Restrictions

Notes: The chart reports the share of respondents in the MS in period t answering that they have heard about prices increasing, as well as retail gasoline price inflation truncated at zero for negative values (labelled in the figure Pos. gas. infl.). Source: University of Michigan, Surveys of Consumers.

2.3 Consumer-level Attributes

The core of our econometric analysis focuses on the connection between consumers' inflation expectations and a number of consumer-level attributes. These can be grouped in the following categories: the current and expected financial situation, consumer attitudes toward major purchases, and the classifications used in the previous literature, namely gender, income and age of the respondent. The attributes are constructed using the survey responses as follows:

Financial situation

- *Financial situation worse*: Individuals responding "worse" to the following question: Would you say that you are better off or worse off financially than you were a year ago? From this category, we exclude all individuals who name high(er) prices as one reason for being worse off, in order to avoid a possible endogeneity bias.

- *Financial expectations worse*: Individuals responding "will be worse off" to the following question: Now looking ahead - do you think that a year from now you will be better off financially, or worse off, or just about the same as now?

10

- *Nominal income expectations worse*: Individuals responding "lower" to the following question: During the next 12 months, do you expect your income to be higher or lower than during the past year?

Purchasing attitudes

- *Time for durable purchases bad*: Individuals responding "bad" to the following question: Generally speaking, do you think now is a good or a bad time for people to buy major household items? Again, to avoid possible endogeneity, we exclude all respondents who respond "Prices are too high, prices going up" to the following question: Why do you say so? (Are there any other reasons?)

- *Time for house purchases bad*: Individuals responding "bad" to the following question: Generally speaking, do you think now is a good time or a bad time to buy a house? Once more, we exclude those who are pessimistic due to high(er) prices.

- *Time for vehicle purchases bad*: Individuals responding "bad" to the following question: Speaking now of the automobile market – do you think the next 12 months or so will be a good time or a bad time to buy a vehicle, such as a car, pickup, van, or sport utility vehicle? Also here, we exclude individuals who give high or rising prices as a reason for their answer.

Other characteristics, following the previous literature

- *Income bottom 20%*: Individuals in the bottom 20% of the income distribution (as identified by the MS).

- *Elderly*: Respondents who are at least 65 years old.

- *Female*: Female respondents.

For each of these categories, we construct a dummy variable that is equal to one in case the attribute applies, and equals zero otherwise. For the financial situation and the purchasing attitudes categories, the dummy variable is equal to one whenever the respondent is "pessimistic", i.e., the consumer describes the current situation as worse, expects a worsening, or perceives the environment as unfavorable for major purchases. For the other characteristics that had been used in the earlier literature, we expect a larger bias for low-income consumers and females, but possibly a smaller one for the elderly.

Notes: The chart reports the share of respondents in the MS in period t answering that the time for purchasing durables / vehicles / houses is bad. Source: University of Michigan, Surveys of Consumers.

Figure 5 gives an impression of the time variation in consumer characteristics, for the example of purchasing attitudes. It reports the share of pessimistic consumers, and demonstrates that this share varies substantially over time. It is apparent that at the end of the sample, with the U.S. economy going through the financial crisis and a major recession, many more consumers felt that times were not good for major purchases.

Table 1 provides a number of summary statistics for each consumer group. The first column reports the number of observations (OBS) for the full sample (which contains 175,147 observations) and separately for each consumer category. The table also provides tests for whether the news reception and the inflation expectations of the various respondent groups are significantly different from those of their peers. These statistics are reported for the percentage of consumers who have heard news about prices ($NEWS_i^P$), the average difference between the MS consumer-specific forecast and the SPF mean inflation forecast (at the time of the survey, $BIAS^F$) and the average difference between the MS consumer-specific forecast and CPI inflation (at the forecast horizon, $BIAS^\pi$).

The bias statistics confirm that consumer inflation expectations are on average upward biased. Relative to actual inflation, the bias for the overall sample amounts to 0.8 percentage points; relative to professional forecasters, consumers overestimate inflation by around half a percentage point. In addition, the magnitude of this bias differs across consumer groups. With the exception of the elderly, differences in the bias are statistically significantly different, and often by large amounts. The biggest difference is found for consumers who expect their financial situation to worsen, with an upward bias that

12

Table 1: Descriptive statistics.

	OBS	OBS(%)	NEWS^P	BIAS$^\pi$	BIAS^F
Overall sample	175,147	100%	4.42	0.78	0.53
Financial situation worse					
Financial situation worse	32,376	18%	3.81***	1.05***	0.85***
Financial expectations worse	19,974	11%	7.29***	1.78***	1.46***
Nominal income expectations worse	22,954	13%	5.02***	1.34***	1.10***
Purchasing attitudes: bad time for					
Durable purchases	27,291	16%	5.26***	1.30***	0.95***
House purchases	34,473	20%	5.51***	1.21***	0.75***
Vehicle purchases	28,068	16%	6.52***	1.41***	1.10***
Others					
Income bottom 20%	24,027	14%	3.45***	1.48***	1.22***
Elderly (Age 65+)	28,336	16%	4.12***	0.74	0.57*
Female	93,356	53%	4.18***	1.13***	0.88***

Notes: The table contains descriptive statistics (columns) conditional on various attributes (rows). OBS: number of uncensored observations; OBS (%): percent of uncensored observations in the overall sample; $NEWS^P$: average percent of consumers observing news; $BIAS^\pi$: average difference between consumers' inflation forecasts and CPI inflation; $BIAS^F$: average difference between consumers' inflation forecasts and the SPF mean inflation forecasts. ***/**/* denotes statistical significance at the 1/5/10% level of the test that each entry is strictly lower than its counterpart computed from the rest of the overall sample with two-sample t-tests (with equal variances). Time period: 1980–2011.

Table 2: Pairwise correlations.

	Financial situation worse			Purchasing att.: bad time for			Others		
	Financial situation	Financial expectations	Nominal expected income	Durable purchases	House purchases	Vehicle purchases	Income bottom 20%	Elderly (Age 65+)	Female
Financial situation worse									
Financial situation	1								
Financial expectations	0.023***	1							
Nominal expected income	0.172***	0.221***	1						
Purchasing attitudes: bad time for									
Durable purchases	0.078***	0.062***	0.071***	1					
House purchases	0.030***	0.066***	0.053***	0.146***	1				
Vehicle purchases	0.046***	0.065***	0.062***	0.257***	0.182***	1			
Others									
Income bottom 20%	0.072***	0.038***	0.022***	0.024***	0.075***	0.037***	1		
Elderly (Age 65+)	-0.028***	0.094***	0.061***	-0.011***	-0.002	-0.004	0.217***	1	
Female	0.035***	-0.004	0.014***	0.034***	0.035***	0.027***	0.117***	0.041***	1

Notes: The table reports pairwise correlations among the variables employed in the regression analysis. *** denotes statistical significance at the 1% level. Time period: 1980–2011.

is around 1 percentage point larger than the one of the other consumers. While these descriptive statistics are unconditional, we will see later on that the differences remain relevant also when we control for other consumer characteristics.

A question that arises is to what extent the various consumer categories that we distinguish are correlated, or in other words whether one can assume that they are reasonably independent to warrant a separate interpretation. Table 2 reports pairwise Pearson correlations among the attributes we include in the analysis. All the correlations are highly statistically significant, but surprisingly small from an economic point of view, with most of them being substantially smaller than 0.1. Based on these results, we will conduct separate regression analyses, using one characteristic at a time, and interpret the results as independent, but it is important to keep in mind that the characteristics are not entirely unrelated.

3   Econometric Framework

This section explains the econometric framework employed in the analysis. We are interested whether the inflation expectations of our consumer groups are more upward biased than those of their peers. For that purpose, we specify the following linear regression model:

$$
\begin{aligned}
BIAS_i &= \alpha_1 + c_i \alpha_2 + NEWS_i^P \alpha_3 + NEWS^N \alpha_4 + \mathbf{x}_i \alpha_5 \\
&\quad + c_i \cdot NEWS_i^P \alpha_6 + c_i \cdot NEWS^N \alpha_7 + u_i, \\
BIAS_i &= \left\{ BIAS_i^\pi, BIAS_i^F \right\},
\end{aligned}
$$
(1)
(2)

where $BIAS_i^\pi$ is the difference between the MS consumer-specific forecast and CPI inflation (at the forecast horizon), and $BIAS_i^F$ is the difference between the MS consumer-specific forecast and the SPF mean inflation forecast. A comparison with actual, realized inflation will tell us about the overall bias of inflation expectations, whereas the comparison with the SPF is meant to compare consumer expectations against a forecast that is in principle conditional on the same information set, namely the information available at the time of the forecast.

α_1 is a constant, c_i denotes the consumer classification of interest, $NEWS_i^P$ is an individual-specific indicator of news perception (which equals one if the interviewee has, in the previous months, heard of recent changes in prices and zero otherwise), and $NEWS^N$ indexes the intensity of news coverage at the time of the survey.[7] $\mathbf{x}_i$ is a vector of socio-

---

[7]In a robustness test, we will also include the last observed CPI inflation rate. We have furthermore considered the possibility that consumers look at alternative inflation measures, such as the average rate of inflation over the six months reinterview period, but did not obtain different results.

economic characteristics (namely gender, age, income, education, race, marital status, location in the United States)[8] and u_i is assumed to be normally distributed. We also interact the consumer classification variable with each of the news intensity measures. While α_2 will reveal whether the various consumer groups differ in their bias, the parameters α_6 and α_7 will reveal whether they differ in their response to news. Note that we omitted time subscripts for simplicity. To assess the statistical significance of our estimates, we calculate robust standard errors using the sandwich estimator.

4 The Determinants of Consumer Inflation Expectations

4.1 Benchmark Results

Having specified the data and the econometric model, we next discuss the econometric results. Tables 3 and 4 confirm the previous findings that consumer inflation expectations are biased upwards. The constant (α_1) reflects the bias of the benchmark consumer, i.e., an agent with the following characteristics: white (non-Hispanic), married, male, 40 years old, high school diploma, an income in the middle quintile of the distribution and living in the North-Center of the country. The bias of the benchmark consumer is estimated to be statistically significant and positive both when we compare inflation expectations against realized inflation in Table 3 (where we find a bias in the order of 0.5 to 0.6 percentage points) and when we compare against those of professional forecasters in Table 4 (with a bias of around 0.3 percentage points).

While the inflation expectations of the representative consumer are biased upwards, the bias is substantially larger for the consumer groups that we study (with the exception of age, where a negative coefficient is in line with the previous literature). The additional bias (α_2) is particularly large for consumers with pessimistic expectations about their financial situation, amounting to 1 additional percentage point. However, also for the other groups, we detect an additional upward bias, which is similar in magnitude to what we find for the consumers in the bottom 20% of the income distribution and slightly smaller than for females. These results hold when comparing consumer inflation expectations to actual inflation and to professional forecasters.

Having heard news about prices (which itself is heavily influenced by positive gasoline

---

[8]Household income is grouped into quintiles and age is measured in integers, while education is split into six groups: *"Grade 0-8, no high school diploma," "Grade 9-12, no high school diploma," "Grade 0-12, with high school diploma," "4 yrs. of college, no degree," "3 yrs. of college, with degree"* and *"4 yrs. of college, with degree."* Race is grouped into *"White except Hispanic," "African-American except Hispanic," "Hispanic," "American Indian or Alaskan Native"* and *"Asian or Pacific Islander,"* while marital status is given as *"Married/with a partner," "Divorced," "Widowed," "Never married."* Finally, the region of residence is grouped into *"West," "North Central," "Northeast," "South."*

Table 3: Determinants of bias relative to actual inflation.

	Financial situation worse			Purchasing attitudes: bad time for			Others		
	Financial situation	Financial expectations	Nominal expected income	Durable purchases	House purchases	Vehicle purchases	Income bottom 20%	Elderly (Age 65+)	Female
HH characteristic (α_2)	0.1486***	1.0905***	0.5010***	0.4384***	0.6169***	0.5692***	0.3875***	-0.3035***	0.6978***
	(0.0293)	(0.0375)	(0.0347)	(0.0318)	(0.0306)	(0.0321)	(0.0462)	(0.0413)	(0.0241)
$NEWS^P$ (α_3)	1.3240***	1.1861***	1.2560***	1.1986***	1.3183***	1.1230***	1.2829***	1.2853***	1.3153***
	(0.0635)	(0.0623)	(0.0626)	(0.0620)	(0.0636)	(0.0638)	(0.0604)	(0.0630)	(0.0741)
$NEWS^P$ * Ch. (α_6)	-0.0596	0.2947*	0.3046*	0.5508***	-0.1304	0.6060***	0.2658	0.1475	-0.0045
	(0.1585)	(0.1600)	(0.1675)	(0.1640)	(0.1464)	(0.1440)	(0.2077)	(0.1635)	(0.1160)
$NEWS^N$ (α_4)	-0.4964***	-0.5150***	-0.4685***	-0.4608***	-0.4265***	-0.4404***	-0.4545***	-0.4010***	-0.4422***
	(0.0191)	(0.0185)	(0.0185)	(0.0189)	(0.0199)	(0.0189)	(0.0185)	(0.0190)	(0.0231)
$NEWS^N$ * Ch. (α_7)	0.0340	-0.0668	-0.1502***	-0.1864***	-0.3996***	-0.2940***	-0.3032***	-0.6398***	-0.0987***
	(0.0418)	(0.0482)	(0.0485)	(0.0418)	(0.0363)	(0.0413)	(0.0528)	(0.0491)	(0.0339)
Constant (α_1)	0.5695***	0.4757***	0.5358***	0.5263***	0.5012***	0.5112***	0.5952***	0.5878***	0.6001***
	(0.0821)	(0.0817)	(0.0819)	(0.0819)	(0.0817)	(0.0819)	(0.0819)	(0.0819)	(0.0819)
Test 1: $\alpha_3+\alpha_6=0$	0.000	0.000	0.000	0.000	0.000	0.000	0.000	0.000	0.000
Test 2: $\alpha_4+\alpha_7=0$	0.000	0.000	0.000	0.000	0.000	0.000	0.000	0.000	0.000
N	175147	175147	175147	175147	175147	175147	175147	175147	175147
Chi^2	3678	4622	3903	3940	4147	4145	3723	3812	3740

Notes: The table reports results based on equation (1), explaining the difference between consumer expectations and actual inflation in $t+12$. All models control for gender, age, income, education, race, marital status, location in the United States. The relevant consumer characteristic is reported in the column header. The definitions of these characteristics are described in Section 2.3. $NEWS^P$ is an individual-specific indicator of news perception (which equals one if the interviewee has heard of recent changes in prices and zero otherwise), $NEWS^N$ indexes the intensity of inflation-related news coverage in the media. $Test\ 1$ denotes p-values of a $Chi^2(1)$ test of $\alpha_3+\alpha_6=0$. $Test\ 2$ denotes p-values of a $Chi^2(1)$ test of $\alpha_4+\alpha_7=0$. N denotes the number of observations. Numbers in parentheses are standard errors. ***/**/* denotes statistical significance at the 1%/5%/10% level. Time period: 1980-2011.

Table 4: Determinants of bias relative to professional forecasts.

	Financial situation worse			Purchasing attitudes: bad time for				Others	
	Financial situation	Financial expectations	Nominal expected income	Durable purchases	House purchases	Vehicle purchases	Income bottom 20%	Elderly (Age 65+)	Female
HH characteristic (α_2)	0.1441***	1.0457***	0.4679***	0.3448***	0.4812***	0.5064***	0.3684***	-0.3125***	0.6899***
	(0.0284)	(0.0360)	(0.0336)	(0.0306)	(0.0294)	(0.0308)	(0.0448)	(0.0396)	(0.0232)
$NEWS^P$ (α_3)	1.2027***	1.0895***	1.1517***	1.1507***	1.1398***	1.0816***	1.1623***	1.2008***	1.1990***
	(0.0584)	(0.0573)	(0.0578)	(0.0578)	(0.0582)	(0.0595)	(0.0555)	(0.0581)	(0.0672)
$NEWS^P$ * Ch. (α_6)	-0.0531	0.1770	0.1849	0.1661	0.1262	0.2929**	0.2593	-0.0997	-0.0145
	(0.1482)	(0.1495)	(0.1543)	(0.1485)	(0.1371)	(0.1314)	(0.1962)	(0.1507)	(0.1070)
$NEWS^N$ (α_4)	-0.8882***	-0.9497***	-0.8685***	-0.8845***	-0.8564***	-0.8721***	-0.8561***	-0.7955***	-0.8513***
	(0.0185)	(0.0178)	(0.0180)	(0.0184)	(0.0193)	(0.0184)	(0.0180)	(0.0184)	(0.0226)
$NEWS^N$ * Ch. (α_7)	-0.1082***	0.0695	-0.2869***	-0.1454***	-0.3202***	-0.2149***	-0.4145***	-0.7904***	-0.1125***
	(0.0404)	(0.0473)	(0.0474)	(0.0406)	(0.0354)	(0.0401)	(0.0508)	(0.0470)	(0.0329)
Constant (α_1)	0.3203***	0.2283***	0.2909***	0.2929***	0.2747***	0.2715***	0.3450***	0.3349***	0.3515***
	(0.0792)	(0.0788)	(0.0790)	(0.0791)	(0.0790)	(0.0790)	(0.0790)	(0.0790)	(0.0791)
Test 1: $\alpha_3+\alpha_6=0$	0.000	0.000	0.000	0.000	0.000	0.000	0.000	0.000	0.000
Test 2: $\alpha_4+\alpha_7=0$	0.000	0.000	0.000	0.000	0.000	0.000	0.000	0.000	0.000
N	175147	175147	175147	175147	175147	175147	175147	175147	175147
Chi^2	6102	7080	6320	6237	6377	6459	6157	6377	6116

Notes: The table reports results based on equation (1), explaining the difference between consumer expectations and the Survey of Professional Forecasters. All models control for gender, age, income, education, race, marital status, location in the United States. The relevant consumer characteristic is reported in the column header. The definitions of these characteristics are described in Section 2.3. $NEWS^P$ is an individual-specific indicator of news perception (which equals one if the interviewee has heard of recent changes in prices and zero otherwise), $NEWS^N$ indexes the intensity of inflation-related news coverage in the media. $Test\ 1$ denotes p-values of a $Chi^2(1)$ test of $\alpha_3 + \alpha_6 = 0$. $Test\ 2$ denotes p-values of a $Chi^2(1)$ test of $\alpha_4 + \alpha_7 = 0$. N denotes the number of observations. ***/**/* denotes statistical significance at the 1%/5%/10% level. Time period: 1980–2011.

inflation) *increases* the bias by around 1.2 to 1.3 percentage points when compared to actual inflation, and by around 1.1 to 1.2 percentage points when compared to professional forecasts (α_3). Interestingly, this effect does not systematically differ across consumer groups (α_6), suggesting that the effect of gasoline price inflation on inflation expectations is universal, and relatively homogeneous across different consumer types.

Contrary to having heard news about prices, more media reporting about inflation tends to *reduce* the bias in inflation expectations (α_4). A one-standard-deviation increase in media reporting (i.e., a change in the index by around 0.8 percentage points), ceteris paribus, leads to a reduction in the bias of around 0.3 to 0.4 percentage points when measured against actual inflation, and of around 0.7 to 0.8 percentage points when measured against the SPF. The effect is estimated to be different across consumer groups (α_7), with a larger reduction in the bias of pessimistic consumers and those in dire financial situations; to give one example, consumers who are pessimistic about house purchases see their bias relative to actual inflation reduced by nearly twice as much as does the average consumer. This result suggests that more news coverage is beneficial in that (i) it reduces the bias in inflation expectations of consumers more generally, and (ii) it does so particularly for those consumer groups that had a larger bias to start with.

4.2 Inflation Expectations During Recessions

In the previous section, we proxied consumers' pessimism by means of their own responses to the MS. Another way to get at consumer pessimism is to test to what extent consumers' forecast accuracy differs during recessions, i.e in times when there is generally less reason for optimism about economic prospects. Accordingly, we have enhanced our econometric model as follows:

$$
\begin{aligned}
BIAS_i \;=\; & \alpha_1 + c_i\alpha_2 + NEWS_i^P\alpha_3 + NEWS^N\alpha_4 + \mathbf{x}_i\alpha_5 + c_iNEWS_i^P\alpha_6 \quad (3) \\
& + c_i \cdot NEWS^N\alpha_7 + NBER\alpha_8 + c_i \cdot NBER\alpha_9 \\
& + NBER \cdot NEWS_i^P\alpha_{10} + NBER \cdot NEWS^N\alpha_{11} + u_i,
\end{aligned}
$$

where $NBER$ is a dummy variable that is equal to one during NBER recessions. This model tests whether the bias in inflation expectations differs during recessions (by means of α_8), whether there is an additional differentiation across consumer groups (α_9), and whether the responsiveness to news changes (α_{10} and α_{11}). The results are reported in Table 5.

A number of findings are noteworthy. First, during recessions, there is a substantial additional upward bias in inflation expectations in the order of 2 percentage points - presumably because consumers underestimate how much inflation tends to drop during

Table 5: Determinants of bias relative to actual inflation, including NBER recessions.

	Financial situation worse			Purchasing attitudes: bad time for				Others	
	Financial situation	Financial expectations	Nominal expected income	Durable purchases	House purchases	Vehicle purchases	Income bottom 20%	Elderly (Age 65+)	Female
HH characteristic (α_2)	0.2256***	0.9576***	0.4986***	0.2581***	0.4586***	0.3392***	0.3171***	-0.2768***	0.6982***
	(0.0307)	(0.0396)	(0.0364)	(0.0344)	(0.0329)	(0.0344)	(0.0480)	(0.0419)	(0.0248)
$NEWS^P$ (α_3)	0.8209***	0.7465***	0.7621***	0.7908***	0.8561***	0.7374***	0.8049***	0.8043***	0.8464***
	(0.0655)	(0.0642)	(0.0650)	(0.0640)	(0.0647)	(0.0654)	(0.0622)	(0.0650)	(0.0744)
$NEWS^P$ * Ch. (α_6)	0.1106	0.1951	0.3994**	0.2975*	-0.1788	0.3699***	0.3053	0.2036	-0.0142
	(0.1560)	(0.1562)	(0.1631)	(0.1601)	(0.1446)	(0.1403)	(0.2038)	(0.1594)	(0.1127)
$NEWS^N$ (α_4)	-0.5136***	-0.5035***	-0.4819***	-0.4728***	-0.3949***	-0.4358***	-0.4574***	-0.4132***	-0.4486***
	(0.0207)	(0.0201)	(0.0203)	(0.0205)	(0.0212)	(0.0205)	(0.0203)	(0.0208)	(0.0246)
$NEWS^N$ * Ch. (α_7)	0.1249***	-0.1049**	-0.0834*	-0.1465***	-0.4900***	-0.3384***	-0.2926***	-0.5828***	-0.0945***
	(0.0420)	(0.0495)	(0.0489)	(0.0425)	(0.0378)	(0.0421)	(0.0529)	(0.0493)	(0.0339)
NBER (α_8)	2.0900***	1.8536***	1.9906***	1.8953***	1.8854***	1.7833***	1.9548***	1.9165***	1.9479***
	(0.2721)	(0.2712)	(0.2721)	(0.2724)	(0.2710)	(0.2715)	(0.2716)	(0.2717)	(0.2717)
NBER * Ch. (α_9)	-0.6518***	0.3028***	-0.2151**	0.1108	0.1644*	0.4562***	0.5107***	-0.1995*	-0.0105
	(0.0870)	(0.1046)	(0.1007)	(0.0846)	(0.0836)	(0.0857)	(0.1391)	(0.1171)	(0.0717)
$NBER * NEWS^P$ (α_{10})	0.8655***	0.8679***	0.9152***	0.8538***	0.9236***	0.8206***	0.8938***	0.8928***	0.8905***
	(0.1358)	(0.1357)	(0.1359)	(0.1367)	(0.1363)	(0.1363)	(0.1359)	(0.1359)	(0.1360)
$NBER * NEWS^N$ (α_{11})	-0.5556***	-0.5455***	-0.5262***	-0.5121***	-0.5269***	-0.5114***	-0.5346***	-0.5221***	-0.5286***
	(0.0391)	(0.0389)	(0.0389)	(0.0390)	(0.0402)	(0.0389)	(0.0389)	(0.0388)	(0.0389)
Constant (α_1)	0.3015***	0.2473***	0.2815***	0.3059***	0.2836***	0.2994***	0.3434***	0.3422***	0.3480***
	(0.0814)	(0.0809)	(0.0811)	(0.0813)	(0.0811)	(0.0813)	(0.0812)	(0.0812)	(0.0813)
Test 1: $\alpha_3+\alpha_6=0$	0.000	0.000	0.000	0.000	0.000	0.000	0.000	0.000	0.000
Test 2: $\alpha_4+\alpha_7=0$	0.000	0.000	0.000	0.000	0.000	0.000	0.000	0.000	0.000
N	175147	175147	175147	175147	175147	175147	175147	175147	175147
Chi^2	6999	7767	7152	7041	7287	7252	6953	7031	6955

Notes: The table reports results based on equation (3), explaining the difference between consumer expectations and actual inflation in $t + 12$. All models control for gender, age, income, education, race, marital status, location in the United States. The relevant consumer characteristic is reported in the column header. The definitions of these characteristics are described in Section 2.3. $NEWS^P$ is an individual-specific indicator of news perception (which equals one if the interviewee has heard of recent changes in prices and zero otherwise), $NEWS^N$ indexes the intensity of inflation-related news coverage in the media. $NBER$ is a dummy variable for recessions. $Test\ 1$ denotes p-values of a $Chi^2(1)$ test of $\alpha_3 + \alpha_6 = 0$. $Test\ 2$ denotes p-values of a $Chi^2(1)$ test of $\alpha_4 + \alpha_7 = 0$. N denotes the number of observations. Numbers in parentheses are standard errors. ***/**/* denotes statistical significance at the 1%/5%/10% level. Time period: 1980–2011.

recessions (or because the pessimism rises). Second, having heard news about prices during recessions substantially increases the bias, by nearly one additional percentage point. Third, additional media reporting is beneficial in the sense that it reduces the bias significantly. Fourth, while some of the interaction terms with our consumer characteristics are statistically significant, they are not consistently significant, and have different signs, such that no clear pattern is emerging. Finally, it is important to note that the results of the previous section all remain valid – the consumer characteristics themselves matter as before, and the way they interact with news about inflation. This suggests that both proxies for pessimism, via the responses in the MS and via the recession dummy, provide us with independent evidence pointing in the same direction.

4.3 Determinants of the Bias

According to Jonung (1981) and Bryan and Venkatu (2001), taking into account demographic characteristics reduces the unexplained bias in the level of consumer forecasts. In this section, we look at the connection between the bias and the set of explanatory variables in the regression models we have considered so far. To this end, we plot the estimated constant terms.

According to Figure 6, when regressing $BIAS_i$ on a constant only, the resulting unconditional bias is around 0.8. When we account for demographics, the bias for the benchmark consumer reduces to about 0.6. Including the NBER recessions reduces this bias further – by about 0.2 – while adding consumer attitudes reduces the unexplained part of the bias to about 0.23, on average. Notably, when accounting for consumers that declare to have negative nominal income expectations, the resulting constant is not statistically different from zero. Overall, the picture emerging from this exercise is that our set of explanatory variables allows compressing the unexplained bias that previous contributions have typically reported.

Figure 6: The unexplained bias in the level of consumer forecasts.

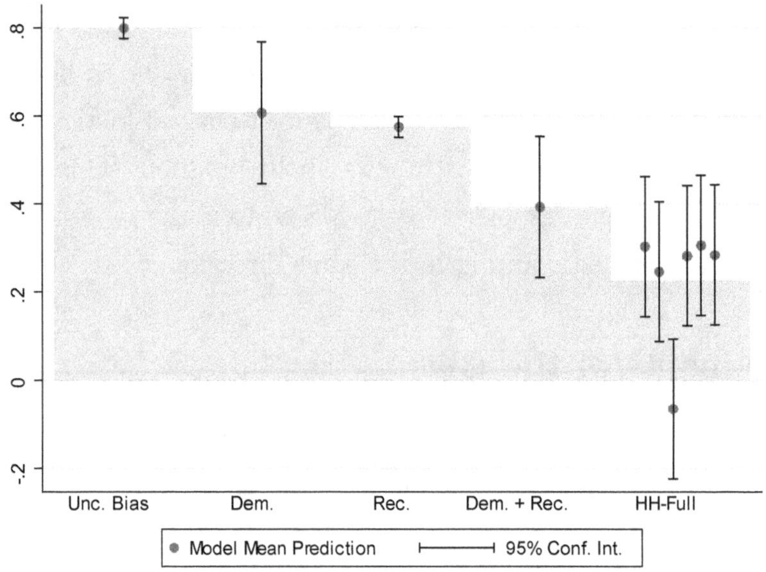

Notes: The chart reports the unexplained bias in the level of consumer forecasts from a model containing: (1) a constant (Unc. Bias); a constant and the demographic characteristics of the representative consumer (Dem.); (2) a constant and the NBER recession dummy (Rec.); (3) a constant, consumers' demographic characteristics and the NBER recession dummy (Dem. + Rec.); (4) a constant, consumers' demographic characteristics, the NBER recession dummy and consumer attitudes (HH-Full). In the last column the height of the shaded area indicates the average of the constants in the models obtained by alternatively including six different types of consumer attitudes.

4.4   Robustness

We have conducted several robustness checks to investigate the sensitivity of our results to our modelling choices. For brevity, we will only show those that relate to the bias of consumers relative to actual inflation (i.e., those reported in Table 3), but results generally hold also for the other analyses. For the first robustness check, we added lagged actual inflation as an explanatory variable to the regression (see Table 6). It turns out that the magnitude of the bias is not responsive to past developments of inflation. Accordingly, all our results go through.[9]

Another robustness test checks for those consumers who are pessimistic about major

---

[9]In an alternative regression, we have also included gasoline price inflation in the set of regressors. However, despite the close connection between hearing news about prices and increases in gasoline prices, the coefficient attached to $NEWS^P$ remains statistically significant and preserves its sign. The same is true when we add consumers' expectations about gasoline price developments based on a question in the MS. As there is substantial item non-response to that particular question, this estimation is based on far fewer observations and therefore not considered as the benchmark regression.

Table 6: Determinants of bias relative to actual inflation, robustness including actual inflation.

	Financial situation worse			Purchasing attitudes: bad time for			Others		
	Financial situation	Financial expectations	Nominal expected income	Durable purchases	House purchases	Vehicle purchases	Income bottom 20%	Elderly (Age 65+)	Female
HH characteristic (α_2)	0.1483***	1.0940***	0.5008***	0.4401***	0.6207***	0.5733***	0.3866***	-0.3037***	0.6978***
	(0.0293)	(0.0375)	(0.0347)	(0.0319)	(0.0309)	(0.0323)	(0.0462)	(0.0413)	(0.0241)
$NEWS^P$ (α_3)	1.3271***	1.2005***	1.2586***	1.2059***	1.3268***	1.1341***	1.2892***	1.2931***	1.3193***
	(0.0639)	(0.0627)	(0.0630)	(0.0624)	(0.0639)	(0.0642)	(0.0609)	(0.0634)	(0.0744)
$NEWS^P$ * Ch. (α_6)	-0.0604	0.2932*	0.3038*	0.5501***	-0.1293	0.6051***	0.2640	0.1454	-0.0046
	(0.1585)	(0.1600)	(0.1675)	(0.1640)	(0.1464)	(0.1440)	(0.2077)	(0.1635)	(0.1160)
Inflation	-0.0029	-0.0139*	-0.0023	-0.0069	-0.0087	-0.0108	-0.0058	-0.0072	-0.0039
	(0.0076)	(0.0076)	(0.0076)	(0.0076)	(0.0077)	(0.0076)	(0.0076)	(0.0075)	(0.0076)
$NEWS^N$ (α_4)	-0.4886***	-0.4789***	-0.4622***	-0.4426***	-0.4054***	-0.4125***	-0.4387***	-0.3814***	-0.4319***
	(0.0243)	(0.0234)	(0.0237)	(0.0236)	(0.0238)	(0.0236)	(0.0237)	(0.0243)	(0.0276)
$NEWS^N$ * Ch. (α_7)	0.0334	-0.0606	-0.1505***	-0.1843***	-0.3937***	-0.2900***	-0.3049***	-0.6415***	-0.0988***
	(0.0418)	(0.0484)	(0.0485)	(0.0419)	(0.0369)	(0.0415)	(0.0528)	(0.0491)	(0.0339)
Constant (α_1)	0.5803***	0.5270***	0.5446***	0.5519***	0.5326***	0.5507***	0.6169***	0.6147***	0.6146***
	(0.0860)	(0.0855)	(0.0858)	(0.0858)	(0.0856)	(0.0857)	(0.0858)	(0.0857)	(0.0858)
Test 1: $\alpha_3+\alpha_6=0$	0.000	0.000	0.000	0.000	0.000	0.000	0.000	0.000	0.000
Test 2: $\alpha_4+\alpha_7=0$	0.000	0.000	0.000	0.000	0.000	0.000	0.000	0.000	0.000
N	175147	175147	175147	175147	175147	175147	175147	175147	175147
Chi^2	3771	4688	3996	4018	4216	4215	3800	3894	3825

Notes: The table reports results based on equation (1), explaining the difference between consumer expectations and actual inflation in $t+12$. All models control for gender, age, income, education, race, marital status, location in the United States. The relevant consumer characteristic is reported in the column header. The definitions of these characteristics are described in Section 2.3. $NEWS^P$ is an individual-specific indicator of news perception (which equals one if the interviewee has heard of recent changes in prices and zero otherwise), $NEWS^N$ indexes the intensity of inflation-related news coverage in the media. $Test$ 1 denotes p-values of a $Chi^2(1)$ test of $\alpha_3+\alpha_6=0$. $Test$ 2 denotes p-values of a $Chi^2(1)$ test of $\alpha_4+\alpha_7=0$. N denotes the number of observations. Numbers in parentheses are standard errors. ***/**/* denotes statistical significance at the 1%/5%/10% level. Time period: 1980–2011.

Table 7: Determinants of bias relative to actual inflation, robustness test for consumer attitudes being determined by rising prices.

	Financial situation, due to prices	Purchasing attitudes: **bad time for**		
		Durable purchases, due to prices	House purchases, due to prices	Vehicle purchases, due to prices
HH characteristic (α_2)	0.6777***	0.7623***	0.5606***	0.5242***
	(0.0255)	(0.0576)	(0.0475)	(0.0344)
$NEWS^P$ (α_3)	1.2075***	1.3309***	1.4019***	1.3774***
	(0.0689)	(0.0599)	(0.0607)	(0.0614)
$NEWS^P$ * Ch. (α_6)	0.1995	-0.4055*	-0.9494***	-0.4859***
	(0.1251)	(0.2380)	(0.2058)	(0.1830)
$NEWS^N$ (α_4)	-0.4530***	-0.4603***	-0.4820***	-0.5043***
	(0.0205)	(0.0181)	(0.0185)	(0.0187)
$NEWS^N$ * Ch. (α_7)	-0.1518***	-0.6609***	-0.2870***	-0.1246***
	(0.0343)	(0.0657)	(0.0537)	(0.0470)
Constant (α_1)	0.3888***	0.5797***	0.5604***	0.5235***
	(0.0821)	(0.0819)	(0.0820)	(0.0821)
Test 1: $\alpha_3+\alpha_6=0$	0.000	0.000	0.021	0.000
Test 2: $\alpha_4+\alpha_7=0$	0.000	0.000	0.000	0.000
N	175147	175147	175147	175147
Chi^2	4575	3846	3782	3871

Notes: The table reports results based on equation (1), explaining the difference between consumer expectations and actual inflation in $t+12$. All models control for gender, age, income, education, race, marital status, location in the United States. The relevant consumer characteristic is reported in the column header, considering consumers that give rising prices as the underlying reason for their assessment. The definitions of these characteristics are described in Section 2.3. $NEWS^P$ is an individual-specific indicator of news perception (which equals one if the interviewee has heard of recent changes in prices and zero otherwise), $NEWS^N$ indexes the intensity of inflation-related news coverage in the media. $Test\ 1$ denotes p-values of a $Chi^2(1)$ test of $\alpha_3+\alpha_6=0$. $Test\ 2$ denotes p-values of a $Chi^2(1)$ test of $\alpha_4+\alpha_7=0$. N denotes the number of observations. ***/**/* denotes statistical significance at the 1%/5%/10% level. Time period: 1980–2011.

Table 8: Determinants of bias relative to actual inflation, robustness test for re-interviewed consumers.

| | Financial situation worse | | | Purchasing attitudes: bad time for | | | Others | | |
	Financial situation	Financial expectations	Nominal expected income	Durable purchases	House purchases	Vehicle purchases	Income bottom 20%	Elderly (Age 65+)	Female
HH characteristic (α_2)	0.0779	0.9348***	0.4321***	0.3288***	0.4791***	0.4777***	0.2681***	-0.3432***	0.3230***
	(0.0474)	(0.0652)	(0.0564)	(0.0526)	(0.0507)	(0.0529)	(0.0742)	(0.0611)	(0.0343)
$NEWS^P$ (α_3)	1.1730***	1.1053***	1.1415***	1.1499***	1.2344***	0.9743***	1.2473***	1.1573***	1.2487***
	(0.1024)	(0.0997)	(0.1007)	(0.0988)	(0.1015)	(0.1014)	(0.0974)	(0.1007)	(0.1164)
$NEWS^P$ * Ch. (α_6)	0.2176	0.2442	0.4101	0.2975	-0.2065	0.8508***	-0.3543	0.2940	-0.0798
	(0.2641)	(0.2840)	(0.2839)	(0.2895)	(0.2517)	(0.2496)	(0.3629)	(0.2833)	(0.1891)
$NEWS^N$ (α_4)	-0.5062***	-0.4677***	-0.4624***	-0.4450***	-0.4105***	-0.4260***	-0.4539***	-0.3796***	-0.4370***
	(0.0287)	(0.0277)	(0.0278)	(0.0286)	(0.0304)	(0.0287)	(0.0277)	(0.0283)	(0.0342)
$NEWS^N$ * Ch. (α_7)	0.1731**	-0.2618***	-0.0958	-0.2081***	-0.3864***	-0.3077***	-0.2187**	-0.6953***	-0.0831
	(0.0700)	(0.0855)	(0.0824)	(0.0697)	(0.0600)	(0.0686)	(0.0854)	(0.0752)	(0.0506)
Constant (α_1)	0.1939	0.1334	0.1536	0.1602	0.1309	0.1391	0.2055*	0.2008	0.2090*
	(0.1247)	(0.1242)	(0.1243)	(0.1243)	(0.1245)	(0.1246)	(0.1243)	(0.1243)	(0.1244)
Test 1: $\alpha_3+\alpha_6=0$	0.000	0.000	0.000	0.000	0.000	0.000	0.011	0.000	0.000
Test 2: $\alpha_4+\alpha_7=0$	0.000	0.000	0.000	0.000	0.000	0.000	0.000	0.000	0.000
Rho	0.959***	0.957***	0.958***	0.958***	0.958***	0.958***	0.958***	0.958***	0.958***
N	71732	71732	71732	71732	71732	71732	71732	71732	71732
Chi^2	885	1122	948	939	999	1013	890	946	896

Notes: The table reports results based on equation (1), explaining the difference between consumer expectations and actual inflation in $t+12$. All models control for gender, age, income, education, race, marital status, location in the United States. The relevant consumer characteristic is reported in the column header. The definitions of these characteristics are described in Section 2.3. $NEWS^P$ is an individual-specific indicator of news perception (which equals one if the interviewee has heard of recent changes in prices and zero otherwise), $NEWS^N$ indexes the intensity of inflation-related news coverage in the media. $Test\ 1$ denotes p-values of a $Chi^2(1)$ test of $\alpha_3+\alpha_6=0$. $Test\ 2$ denotes p-values of a $Chi^2(1)$ test of $\alpha_4+\alpha_7=0$. N denotes the number of observations. Rho denotes the coefficient on the residuals of the selection equation in the main regression (which also includes in the set of regressors some interaction terms between different consumers' socio-demographic characteristics). Numbers in parentheses are standard errors. ***/**/* denotes statistical significance at the 1%/5%/10% level.

Table 9: Determinants of bias relative to actual inflation, robustness test excluding $NEWS^P$.

	Financial situation worse			Purchasing attitudes: bad time for			Others		
	Financial situation	Financial expectations	Nominal expected income	Durable purchases	House purchases	Vehicle purchases	Income bottom 20%	Elderly (Age 65+)	Female
HH characteristic (α_2)	0.1382***	1.1458***	0.5244***	0.4783***	0.6276***	0.6348***	0.3912***	-0.3052***	0.6928***
	(0.0290)	(0.0367)	(0.0342)	(0.0315)	(0.0301)	(0.0315)	(0.0460)	(0.0411)	(0.0239)
$NEWS^N$ (α_4)	-0.4883***	-0.5074***	-0.4584***	-0.4522***	-0.4186***	-0.4302***	-0.4455***	-0.3912***	-0.4362***
	(0.0191)	(0.0185)	(0.0185)	(0.0190)	(0.0199)	(0.0190)	(0.0186)	(0.0190)	(0.0231)
$NEWS^N$ * Ch. (α_7)	0.0390	-0.0669	-0.1593***	-0.1826***	-0.4007***	-0.3046***	-0.3018***	-0.6450***	-0.0928***
	(0.0418)	(0.0482)	(0.0486)	(0.0418)	(0.0363)	(0.0413)	(0.0528)	(0.0491)	(0.0340)
Constant (α_1)	0.6168***	0.5117***	0.5777***	0.5643***	0.5438***	0.5445***	0.6393***	0.6318***	0.6452***
	(0.0823)	(0.0819)	(0.0822)	(0.0822)	(0.0820)	(0.0821)	(0.0822)	(0.0821)	(0.0822)
Test 1: $\alpha_4+\alpha_7=0$	0.000	0.000	0.000	0.000	0.000	0.000	0.000	0.000	0.000
N	175147	175147	175147	175147	175147	175147	175147	175147	175147
Chi^2	3131	4147	3369	3421	3596	3651	3178	3273	3158

Notes: The table reports results based on equation (1), explaining the difference between consumer expectations and actual inflation in $t+12$. All models control for gender, age, income, education, race, marital status, location in the United States. The relevant consumer characteristic is reported in the column header. The definitions of these characteristics are described in Section 2.3. $NEWS^N$ indexes the intensity of inflation-related news coverage in the media. $Test$ 1 denotes p-values of a $Chi^2(1)$ test of $\alpha_4 + \alpha_7 = 0$. N denotes the number of observations. Numbers in parentheses are standard errors. ***/**/* denotes statistical significance at the 1%/5%/10% level. Time period: 1980–2011.

purchases, or see themselves in a difficult financial situation, but who mention that this is due to increasing prices (whereas, so far, these had been excluded from the consumer groups). Of course, we would expect these consumers to have a substantially larger bias, and this is indeed the case, as shown in Table 7. The exception is consumers who think that it's a bad time to purchase a house due to prices – which is intuitive, since these respondents most likely have house prices in mind when answering that question, so they need not have a larger bias with regard to consumer prices. All other results go through with this robustness test – perceived news increases the bias, and media reporting decreases it, and particularly so for the pessimistic consumers.

A third robustness test is concerned with the fact that around 40% of the consumers in the MS get re-interviewed. The response behavior of these re-interviewed consumers has been studied by Anderson (2008) and Madeira and Zafar (2012), and seems to be characterized by some learning over time. Accordingly, it is interesting to restrict the analysis to re-interviewed consumers only, as their inflation expectations might be less biased than those of the entire sample.[10] While the overall bias does indeed shrink somewhat when comparing Table 8 to Table 3, we still find an elevated bias for our selected consumer groups; as well, the responsiveness to news is qualitatively unchanged.

Our benchmark model contains a variable that indicates whether a respondent has heard news about prices. Our fourth robustness test drops this variable, $NEWS_i^P$, with results reported in Table 9. The estimated coefficients change only marginally, while qualitatively all results remain intact, suggesting that both news variables exert independent effects on inflation expectations.

Finally, one might wonder whether the effect would be more prominent had we only included respondents who have heard news about rising prices. As discussed earlier, most of the observations for this variable originate from respondents who have heard about rising prices, whereas very few report to have heard about declining prices. Replacing our variable for perceived news to include only news about rising prices does not alter our results (which are not shown, for brevity).

5   Conclusions

What are the determinants of consumers' inflation-forecast errors? This paper has used the microdata of the Surveys of Consumers to shed further light on this important question. While it is well known that a number of socio-economic characteristics such as gender, age or income affect inflation expectations, we have shown that the same also

---

[10]From a total of 71,629 re-interviews, we lose 6.3% of observations due to question attrition (i.e., 4,513 individuals decided not to provide a year-ahead inflation expectation). This may represent a potential source of bias. In order to account for question attrition, we implement the Heckman correction (Heckman, 1979), a procedure that offers a means of correcting for non-randomly selected samples.

holds true for consumer attitudes. Having pessimistic attitudes – for example, toward the purchase of durables or homes, experiencing or expecting financial difficulties, as well as expectations that household income will go down in the future – affects inflation expectations in substantially, increasing the upward bias that is anyway inherent in consumer inflation expectations. The effects are not only statistically significant, they are substantial in magnitude, and thus help explain time variation in the evolution of consumer inflation expectations.

Generally, consumer inflation expectations are highly sensitive to perceived news about rising prices, which themselves are tightly connected to the evolution of gasoline prices. Rising gasoline prices are noticed much more than falling gasoline prices, and they lead consumers to revise their expectations more frequently, but worsen their bias. This is in contrast to media reporting about inflation. More intense media reporting lowers the bias, and especially so for pessimistic consumers and consumers in dire financial situations.

The findings have important implications for policy-makers. They suggest that more communication about inflation improves consumers' inflation expectations, and particularly so for consumers who are in the right tail of the distribution, i.e., those who have a particularly strong upward bias.

References

ANDERSON, R. D. J. (2008): "US Consumer Inflation Expectations: Evidence Regarding Learning, Accuracy and Demographics," University of Manchester Discussion Paper 2008/099, University of Manchester.

ARMANTIER, O., S. NELSON, G. TOPA, W. VAN DER KLAAUW, AND B. ZAFAR (2012): "The price is right: updating of inflation expectations in a randomized price information experiment," Staff Reports 543, Federal Reserve Bank of New York.

BAUMEISTER, R., E. BRATSLAVSKY, C. FINKENAUER, AND K. VOHS (2001): "Bad is stronger than good," *Review of General Psychology*, 5, 323–370.

BLINDER, A. S., AND A. B. KRUEGER (2004): "What Does the Public Know about Economic Policy, and How Does It Know It?," *Brookings Papers on Economic Activity*, 35(2004-1), 327–397.

BRYAN, M. F., AND G. VENKATU (2001): "The demographics of inflation opinion surveys," *Economic Commentary*, (15).

CAPISTRAN, C., AND A. TIMMERMANN (2009): "Disagreement and Biases in Inflation Expectations," *Journal of Money, Credit and Banking*, 41(2-3), 365–396.

CARROLL, C. D. (2003): "Macroeconomic Expectations Of Households and Professional Forecasters," *The Quarterly Journal of Economics*, 118(1), 269–298.

CHRISTENSEN, C., P. ELS, AND M. ROOIJ (2006): "Dutch Households' Perceptions of Economic Growth and Inflation," *De Economist*, 154(2), 277–294.

COIBION, O., AND Y. GORODNICHENKO (2010): "Information Rigidity and the Expectations Formation Process: A Simple Framework and New Facts," NBER Working Papers 16537, National Bureau of Economic Research, Inc.

———— (2015): "Is the Phillips Curve Alive and Well after All? Inflation Expectations and the Missing Disinflation," *American Economic Journal: Macroeconomics*, 7(1), 197–232.

CURTIN, R. (1996): "Procedure to estimate price expectations," Mimeo, University of Michigan.

———— (2013): "Survey of Consumers," Discussion paper, Survey Reserach Center, University of Michigan.

DEL GIOVANE, P., S. FABIANI, AND R. SABBATINI (2009): "What's Behind 'Inflation Perceptions'? A Survey-Based Analysis of Italian Consumers," *Giornale degli Economisti*, 68(1), 25–52.

EASAW, J., R. GOLINELLI, AND M. MALGARINI (2013): "What determines households inflation expectations? Theory and evidence from a household survey," *European Economic Review*, 61(C), 1–13.

FRIEDRICH, C. (2014): "Global Inflation Dynamics in the Post-Crisis Period: What Explains the Twin Puzzle?," Working Papers 14-36, Bank of Canada.

GEORGANAS, S., P. J. HEALY, AND N. LI (2014): "Frequency bias in consumers? perceptions of inflation: An experimental study," *European Economic Review*, 67(C), 144–158.

HECKMAN, J. J. (1979): "Sample Selection Bias as a Specification Error," *Econometrica*, 47(1), 153–61.

JONUNG, L. (1981): "Perceived and Expected Rates of Inflation in Sweden," *American Economic Review*, 71(5), 961–68.

KAHNEMAN, D., AND A. TVERSKY (1979): "Prospect Theory: An Analysis of Decision under Risk," *Econometrica*, 47(2), 263–91.

LAMLA, M. J., AND T. MAAG (2012): "The Role of Media for Inflation Forecast Disagreement of Households and Professionals," *Journal of Money, Credit and Banking*, 44(7), 1325–1350.

LOMBARDELLI, C., AND J. SALEHEEN (2003): "Public expectations of UK inflation," *Bank of England Quarterly Bulletin*, 43, 281–290.

MADEIRA, C., AND B. ZAFAR (2012): "Heterogeneous Inflation Expectations and Learning," Federal Reserve Bank of New York Staff Report 536, Federal Reserve Bank of New York.

MALGARINI, M. (2009): "Quantitative Inflation Perceptions and Expectations of Italian Consumers," *Giornale degli Economisti*, 68(1), 53–80.

MALMENDIER, U., AND S. NAGEL (2013): "Learning from Inflation Experiences," Mimeo, UC Berkeley and Stanford University.

MENZ, J.-O., AND P. POPPITZ (2013): "Households' disagreement on inflation expectations and socioeconomic media exposure in Germany," Discussion Papers 27/2013, Deutsche Bundesbank, Research Centre.

PFAJFAR, D., AND E. SANTORO (2009): "Asymmetries in Inflation Expectations Across Sociodemographic Groups," Mimeo, Tilburg University.

——— (2013): "News on Inflation and the Epidemiology of Inflation Expectations," *Journal of Money, Credit and Banking*, 45(6), 1045–1067.

RANYARD, R., F. D. MISSIER, N. BONINI, D. DUXBURY, AND B. SUMMERS (2008): "Perceptions and expectations of price changes and inflation: A review and conceptual framework," *Journal of Economic Psychology*, 29(4), 378–400.

SIMS, C. A. (2003): "Implications of rational inattention," *Journal of Monetary Economics*, 50(3), 665–690.

SNIR, A., AND D. LEVY (2011): "Shrinking Goods and Sticky Prices: Theory and Evidence," Working Paper Series 17/11, The Rimini Centre for Economic Analysis.

SOULELES, N. S. (2004): "Expectations, Heterogeneous Forecast Errors, and Consumption: Micro Evidence from the Michigan Consumer Sentiment Surveys," *Journal of Money, Credit and Banking*, 36(1), 39–72.

TVERSKY, A., AND D. KAHNEMAN (1974): "Judgment under uncertainty: Heuristics and biases," *Science*, 185, 1124–1131.

WEBLEY, P., AND R. SPEARS (1986): "Economic preferences and inflationary expectations," *Journal of Economic Psychology*, 7(3), 359–369.